LIFE SCIENCE

SENSES

Patricia Miller-Schroeder

WEIGL PUBLISHERS INC.

Project Coordinator
Heather C. Hudak

Design
Bryan Pezzi

Cover Design
Terry Paulhus

Published by Weigl Publishers Inc.
350 5th Avenue, Suite 3304, PMB 6G
New York, NY 10118-0069

Website: www.weigl.com

All of the Internet URLs given in the book were valid at the time of
publication. However, due to the dynamic nature of the Internet, some
addresses may have changed, or sites may have ceased to exist since
publication. While the author and publisher regret any inconvenience
this may cause readers, no responsibility for any such changes can be
accepted by either the author or the publisher.

Library of Congress Cataloging-in-Publication Data

Miller-Schroeder, Patricia.
  Senses / Patricia Miller-Schroeder.
    p. cm. -- (Life science)
  Includes bibliographical references and index.
  ISBN 978-1-59036-715-5 (hard cover : alk. paper) -- ISBN 978-1-
59036-716-2 (soft cover : alk. paper)
  1. Senses and sensation--Juvenile literature. I. Title.
  QP434.M558 2008
  612.8--dc22
                                    2007012636

Printed in the United States of America
1 2 3 4 5 6 7 8 9 0 11 10 09 08 07

Every reasonable effort has been made to trace ownership and to
obtain permission to reprint copyright material. The publishers would
be pleased to have any errors or omissions brought to their attention
so that they may be corrected in subsequent printings.

Contents

What Do You Know about Senses?

When we listen to music, lick an ice-cream cone, or pet a kitten, our senses give us important information. We rely on our noses, eyes, ears, tongues, and skin to tell us about our world. These parts of the body are our **sense organs**. They let us smell, see, hear, taste, and touch things.

■ Like puppies, kittens are born with their eyes closed. Kittens cannot see for at least 10 days after birth.

All people and animals have sense organs, but they begin working at different times. Hearing often works right away. The sense of sight can take longer. Most human babies can see things clearly by the time they are six months old.

■ Spiders are born with all of their senses working.

Activity

Sensing an Apple

An apple gives you a chance to use all of your senses. Look at it carefully. Record as much information about the apple as possible. What is its size, shape, and color? Does it have bruises, a stem, leaves? Is it shiny? How does it smell and feel? Bite into it. What sounds do you hear? How does it taste?

5

Sense Organs

The major sense organs in the human body are the nose, eyes, ears, tongue, and skin. Each sense organ has a special job to do and gives us different information about the world.

■ Our sense of smell can alert us if animals are nearby. A skunk's strong smell drives humans away.

How do the sense organs work? Each one has special cells called **receptor cells**. Receptor cells are like spies. When they detect something, they send messages to the brain. The brain then lets us know what is affecting us.

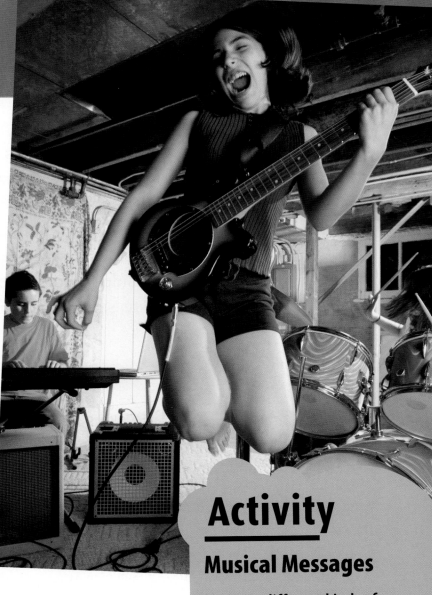

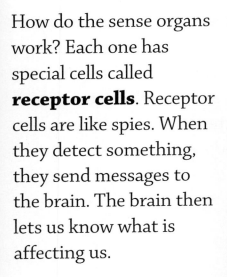

Activity

Musical Messages

Listen to different kinds of music. Your brain will send messages to you about the music. Draw what you "see" in your mind as you listen.

■ You know what to watch out for when you see certain signs and pictures. In some parts of the world, people must watch out for camels crossing the road!

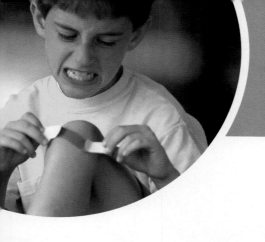

How Many Senses Do You Have?

Many scientists say humans have nine or more senses. Our **internal senses** tell us about the body and what it needs. The internal senses are **balance**, pain, hunger, and thirst. Our **external senses** tell us about the outside world. The external senses are hearing, taste, sight, touch, and smell.

Internal Senses

Balance	Pain	Hunger	Thirst	Hearing
The sense of balance keeps us from falling down.	The sense of pain lets us know when we are hurt.	The sense of hunger tells us when to eat.	The sense of thirst tells us when to drink.	The sense of hearing helps us hear soft and loud sounds.

Puzzler

1. What clues can the body send you if it needs food?

2. What clue can the body send you if it is off balance?

Taste	Sight	Touch	Smell
The sense of taste lets us enjoy the food we eat.	The sense of sight helps us identify friends.	Touch helps us decide if an object is hard or soft.	Smell helps us identify the scent of a flower.

9

Hearing

Ears are the sense organs that help us hear. **Sound waves** in the air strike the outer ear on the side of your head. The outer ear is shaped like a cone. It bounces the waves into your ear through a small tunnel. This tunnel is called the **auditory canal**. A thin layer of skin called the **eardrum** stretches across the canal. The sound waves beat on the eardrum and make it **vibrate**. The inner ear detects the vibrations and sends a message to the brain. The brain receives the message from the ear and tells us whether the sound is loud or soft, musical or shrill. The brain tries to identify the sound for us.

■ **The ear has many small parts that help collect and sense sound waves.**

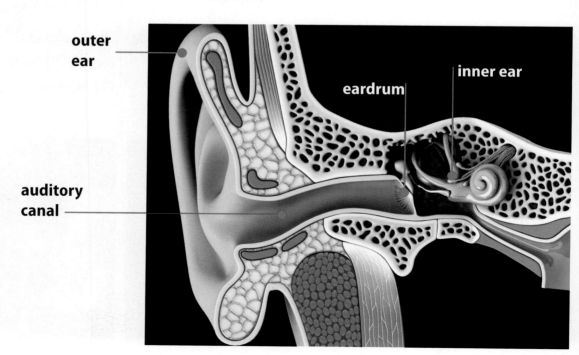

outer ear

auditory canal

eardrum

inner ear

■ The strings of a piano send out sounds that are high and low in pitch.

■ Ear protectors can help protect our ears from harmful loud noises.

Activity

Hearing Aid

Sound becomes louder when sound waves travel in only one direction. Roll a piece of paper into a cone shape. Speak into the narrow end. The cone makes the sound waves from your voice travel out in one direction. Your voice sounds louder. If you wrapped the paper in a cone shape around your outer ear, what would this do to the sounds you hear?

Seeing

The eye sends messages to the brain that roses and tulips look different from each other.

Eyes are the sense organs that help us see. The receptors in the back of the eyes detect light. They change the light into messages to the brain about the shape, size, and color of objects. The eyes also pick up if something is dim or bright. The brain, working with the eye, helps people decide whether something is safe or harmful, pretty or ugly.

■ Our eyes can fool us. Spots on baby deer help them blend in with plants, so enemies cannot see them.

■ Falcons have great eyesight. They can see other birds flying 1,000 feet (305 meters) below them.

Activity

Looking for Colors

Look around, and see how many colors you can identify in one minute. Ask a friend to time you.

Smelling

The nose is the sense organ that helps us smell. The inside of the nose is called the **nasal cavity**. Scents that reach the nose travel inside the nasal cavity. Receptor cells deep inside the nasal cavity pick out different smells.

■ Butterflies use smells to send signals to other butterflies. Special wing scales release these smells.

■ Pigs have poor eyesight, but their sense of smell is very good. They can even smell food buried underground.

The receptor cells send messages to the brain. The brain helps us decide if a smell is pleasing or displeasing. Some smells may be fruity, flowery, or spicy. Others might be smoky, sour, or moldy.

■ The smell of food in landfills sometimes attracts bears. They visit the landfills at night to find food.

15

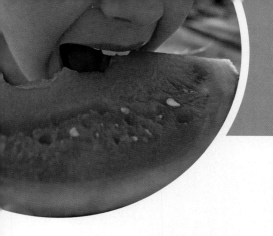

Tasting

The tongue is the sense organ that helps us taste. Tiny receptors called **taste buds** are located on the tongue. Taste buds detect certain flavors and send messages to the brain. The brain tells us if the taste is salty, sweet, bitter, sour, or spicy. The brain lets us know if something tastes good.

Sweet foods

Sweet foods, like chocolate and cherries, can make our mouths water. Sweet foods include cookies, cakes, marshmallows, and ice cream. Taste buds on the tip of the tongue help detect sweetness in foods. Sugar is usually what makes foods sweet.

Spicy foods

Spicy foods, such as chili peppers, can make us feel like our mouths are on fire. Taste buds all over the tongue detect spicy food. The more often people eat spicy foods, the more their sense of taste becomes used to them. People who eat spicy foods all the time must put large amounts of hot pepper in their food to keep it tasting spicy.

The sense of taste works with the sense of smell. Messages about the foods we eat come from the brain and from the senses of taste and smell working together.

Activity

Tasting Lemonade

Make lemonade by mixing 4 cups (1,000 mL) of water with 6 tablespoons (90 mL) of lemon juice and 12 tablespoons (180 mL) of sugar. Taste the lemonade, and write down whether it is sweet or bitter. Pour some lemonade into three different glasses. Add more lemon to one, more water to another, and more sugar to the last one. Write down how each tastes. Which one tastes best?

Sour foods

Sour foods, such as lemons and limes, make our mouths pucker. The taste buds that help detect sour tastes are on either side of the tongue at the back.

Bitter foods

Bitter foods, such as coffee and dark chocolate, can leave a sharp, unpleasant taste in the mouth. The taste buds at the very back of the tongue help tell us if a food tastes bitter.

Salty foods

Salty foods, like potato chips and salted nuts, make us thirsty. The more salty foods we eat, the more we need to drink. The taste buds that help tell us if foods are salty are on either side of the tongue at the front.

17

Touching

The skin that covers our bodies is the sense organ that lets us experience touch. There are many receptors in the skin. Some send messages to the brain about whether the skin feels hot or cold. Other receptors send messages about things touching the skin lightly or painfully. The brain helps us decide what to do. We may want to put on or take off clothing to feel warmer or cooler. We will want to move away from what is hurting or bothering us.

■ You can feel a mosquito when it touches one of the many small hairs on your skin.

■ People wear warm clothing in the winter so that they do not feel cold.

We have many touch receptors in our hands and fingertips. These let us touch objects and feel their **texture**. We can tell if they are hard or soft, smooth or rough, flat or bumpy.

■ **Seals and other mammals have whiskers that help them discover how big a space is.**

Activity

A Texture Picture

Find items that have different textures, and glue them onto a piece of cardboard. You may want to use paper strips, plastic buttons, egg cartons, bottle caps, cloth pieces, or dry leaves. You can probably think of many more objects to add.

■ **Cactus plants have sharp spikes that stop animals from eating them.**

Senses Gone Wild

People and animals sense some things in the world differently. Humans have hands to carry things, but elephants have to use their trunks to move things around.

Humans cannot see electrical currents in the air, but some insects and birds can. Some birds, such as owls, can even see in the dark.

■ Most people can see in color, but dogs can only see in shades of gray. They have a stronger sense of smell that helps them discover things humans cannot detect.

■ An elephant's trunk is amazing. It can carry a log that weighs 600 pounds (272 kilograms), but it can also pick up a quarter.

People use the sense of sight mostly to help them get around, but bats need more than their sight when flying. If bats cannot hear well, they will crash when flying.

■ Snakes and people have very different senses. Can you smell through your tongue? Snakes can.

Have you ever watched a butterfly fly from flower to flower? Why does it do this?

Answer: The butterfly finds its food by sensing the sweetness of flowers with its feet.

21

Expanding Our Senses

Humans are curious creatures. Since there are limits to our senses, we try to expand them. We have watched animals and developed machines to copy how they talk under water or see far away. Some of these machines are microscopes, telescopes, and **sonar**.

■ Microscopes and telescopes are two machines that give us keen sight like birds. Microscopes let us see tiny objects. Telescopes let us see things far away.

Sonar machines send out sound waves through water in order to find objects. The sound waves travel until they reach and bounce off something. Some of the waves return to the sonar machine. The person operating the machine can then find the object by tracing the path of the sound waves.

■ Fishing boats use sonar to search for fish in lakes and oceans. Dolphins find food by using their natural sonar.

Activity

Looking at Water

Examine a drop of water from a puddle under a microscope. Record what you see.

23

What Are Some "Sensational" Careers?

Optometrists help people with eye health. They give eye exams and let people know if they need eyeglasses or contact lenses. To be an optometrist, you must attend a university to learn how to test eyesight. After completing the necessary courses, you will need a license to practice optometry. Then, you will be able to help people who are having trouble seeing.

■ **Optometrists help people see better.**

There are other careers that involve the senses. Massage therapists help people relax. They use the sense of touch in their work. Cooks hope people will like the smell, taste, and sight of the tasty food they make.

Activity

Do Your Own Research

Ask a parent or teacher to help you find information about these careers that relate to the senses.

- artist
- brain surgeon
- candle maker
- cook
- dentist
- ear, nose, and throat doctor
- massage therapist
- musician

Coping with Lost Senses

Sometimes, people are born with a sense organ that does not work properly. We have created tools to help our senses. If our eyesight needs improvement, we can wear glasses or contact lenses. They help us focus.

If we lose all or some of our hearing, a hearing aid may help. A hearing aid is usually worn in the ear. It picks up sound waves and makes them loud enough to set off receptors inside the ear.

■ **Many American Sign Language symbols express complete thoughts rather than single words.**

Losing one of the senses can be difficult. People who have lost one sense often depend more on their other senses. For example, people who cannot see often develop very good senses of touch and hearing. They can also extend their sense of touch with canes and seeing-eye dogs. People who cannot hear use sign language to communicate.

Sign Language Alphabet

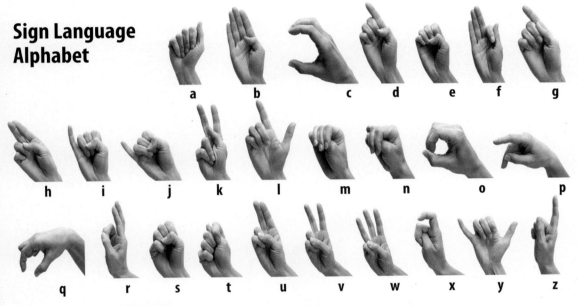

■ Difficult words and names are spelled out in sign language, using hand signals in place of letters.

Puzzler

How do people who are seeing impaired read?

Answer: Many seeing impaired people read by using **braille.** Braille uses raised dots that seeing impaired people can feel with their fingertips. It was invented 150 years ago by a seeing impaired teacher, Louis Braille.

Be Sensible with Your Senses

People should be careful with their senses because they can be hurt or lost. Accidents, working, and having fun can injure senses. Working for a long time around loud noises can harm a person's hearing.

■ **Using headphones to listen to very loud music can damage your ears after a while.**

■ **Sun reflecting off snow can cause seeing impairment.**

How can you protect your senses?

1. Know how hot your food is before you put it in your mouth. Taste buds are easily damaged by too much heat.

2. Do not stare at the Sun, even during a beautiful sunset. The light is bright enough to damage your eyes.

3. Keep all your skin well covered if you are outside in freezing weather. If your skin freezes, you may lose the skin or its ability to sense touch.

4. Put your hands over your ears if you must be near a loud noise. Do not stay there. Try to leave as soon as you can.

Go on a Sense Safari

Imagine you are going for a walk outdoors with a group of friends. Here are pictures of things you might see on your safari. Link the objects in each picture with the senses you would most likely use to explore them. You can sense a bee safely by hearing it and seeing it. You would not want to touch it!

You can sense a piece of fruit with all of your senses except hearing. It would be difficult to hear a grape. Exploring the world with all of your senses can be exciting.

Smell

See

Hear

Taste

Touch

31

Glossary

auditory canal: tunnel from the outer ear to the inner ear

balance: steadiness

braille: system of writing and reading using raised dots instead of letters

eardrum: a very thin wall between the outer and inner ear

external senses: the senses of hearing, taste, sight, touch, and smell

internal senses: the senses of balance, pain, hunger, and thirst

nasal cavity: the inside of the nose

receptor cells: small units in sense organs that send messages to the brain when set off

sense organs: different parts of the body that take in information from their surroundings

sonar: a machine that sends out sound waves that bounce off underwater objects

sound waves: the waves in air and water caused by vibrations

taste buds: receptors found on the tongue that detect chemicals in food

texture: the way something feels

vibrate: move back and forth quickly

Index

Websites

www.afb.org/braillebug/braille_deciphering.asp
www.masterstech-home.com/ASLDict.html

www.hhmi.org/senses
http://hes.ucf.k12.pa.us/gclaypo/senses

Some websites stay current longer than others. For further websites, use your search engines to locate topics such as Louis Braille, common sense, intuition, sonar, and telephone.